Endless Path of Time

Worley Faver

SeaDog Press
Lake City, Florida 32024

All rights reserved. No part of this book may be reproduced, or stored in a retrieval system, or transmitted in any form or by any means, electronic, mechanical, photocopying, recording, or otherwise without express written permission except by a reviewer who may quote brief passages in review.

Cover design: SeaDog Press

Editor: Florence Love Karsner

Copyright© 2022 Worley Faver

ISBN: 978-1-943369-19-5

Dedication Page

This book is dedicated to Dena Hughes Faver – my wife, best friend, mother of my children, and the most beautiful soul I have been blessed to know during this incarnation!

Table of Contents

Wabi 1

Young Samuel 5

Travels 9

The Guana 21

The Legend of Connie 25

Imagination 29

Milton 33

Trailer Trash 37

God Bless Our Police Officers 39

Bragging Rights 43

The Farm Doctor 47

The Mountain Sorcerer 49

Palm Valley Winter School Days 53

Birdie 55

Dreams 59

Angels 63

My Therapy 65

Preface

I will be eighty-five years old this year, and looking back to the beginning of this path I find there have been some experiences that cry out to be shared with my family and friends.

These stories are all true except for the first one, entitled "Wabi." This myth is likely to reflect—as most myths do—a kernel of truth. It attempts to reconstruct how Palm Valley and the Guana Preserve may have appeared 600 years ago and comes mostly from my imagination.

The other true stories reflect the changing world over these many years and my interaction with events that occurred in my life. I apologize for the apparent random way my stories are grouped. As you will see, the stories are not presented in any apparent order, chronological or otherwise. I enjoy telling old stories as they come to this old mind.

Acknowledgements

What a wonderful experience it is to have the opportunity to work with the best publisher and editor in the world of stories and books. My publisher, CAPT Garry Karsner, Supply Corps, USNR (Ret), and editor and author, Florence Love Karsner, made the whole writing endeavor a pleasure for this old storyteller. They displayed incredible patience, expertise, and untiring effort in helping me create these stories. It was truly a joy to be exposed to their intelligence and good humor. Without their encouragement and friendship, this project would have been impossible.

Prologue

These stories reflect the long life of a man blessed to have been born and raised in the South. This life has been full of happiness, amusement, and of course some tears of sadness and joy. It has also been filled with interesting people and events which occurred surrounding our intertwined lives.

Kevin Faver's Introduction

It was still dark when Dad was loading up the boat. Rods, reels, a five-gallon bucket for our live bait and an anchor. As we idled away from the dock, the sun was just showing itself.

The boat was no more than fifteen feet and the little outboard was probably a 5 hp. I sat in the front of the small boat anticipating the fish we would catch. I saw channel marker 3, then 5, 8, 12 knowing all along where we would fish. Even though I was only eight years old I knew where we were going. We were headed to marker 15, Dad's favorite spot.

When we arrived, Dad would ease us into position and I would slide out the anchor. Dad loved to float fish so we always had a rod rigged with a slip cork. I never let him know, but to this day float fishing is still my favorite! There was ample time between bites so the conversation always led to Dad's stories or his teachings. He would tell me stories of The Big House, crazy deer running around in Palm Valley, and of course stories of Guana, which is now a state park. I would listen intently, all the while watching my rod.

As I got older, I became a part of some of his stories. We hunted, fished, rode horses, and raised cattle in Guana. This piece of land was part of our soul. I'm privileged to have shared times with Dad on the water, in the woods, and on the tailgate lunches on the old Chevy truck—lunches that always included a ham sandwich, a piece of fruit and of course an RC Cola. I've heard most of these stories dozens of times and can't wait to hear them again. Thanks for all your wisdom, Daddy, and thank you for sharing your stories!

Capt. Kevin

Keith Faver's Introduction

When my father asked me to write an introduction to his latest book of short stories, I locked up. Felt painfully inadequate. How could I possibly introduce a man who has been my superhero forever? A man with the sharpest intellect of anyone I have ever met. A man who consistently sacrificed personally for the betterment of his family. A man with a work ethic—even now at eighty-five—that continues to astonish all of us who know and love him.

My father is now the oldest, native-born, life-long resident of Palm Valley, a slice of old North Florida swampland slowly-turned, prime real estate since the intracoastal waterway bisected it in the early part of the last century. Thanks to Dad's amazing memory, my brother, Kevin, and my sister, Cindy, and I never had to imagine what it was like for our father growing up in Palm Valley in the 1930's and 40's. His memories are photographic, specific and sharp. He remembers not only every relative and person who lived here, but also the most important stories of each of their lives.

When we look back on our childhood in Palm Valley, we remember a mysterious place. Oak trees overhanging every road, making each memory a darkening world. The road was curvier then and the Valley's inhabitants fewer. But you always waved when you saw someone. Literally they were either a friend or you were related to them. I can see my brother, Kevin, riding his bike down Roscoe Boulevard, shotgun across the handlebars, heading to hunt wood ducks. I rode a mini-bike to school in 6th grade, straight through the woods. Unimaginable now.

My father is a gifted artist with a brilliant mind who never fails to tell us he loves us. He's a hugger. He was our personal Google. And the stories he is sharing give us a forever gift of all he is.

Enjoy!
Keith

Wabi

His name was Wabi and he sat on the edge of the Tolomato River salt marsh—not moving at all—just thinking. He remembered the humans arrived about 12,000 years ago; then the Timucua in their dugout cypress canoes, and much later the Spanish explored the river outfitted in their armor, swords, pikes, and firearms. Later, the British spent twenty years trying to tame the land with plantation crops, canals, and coquina-lined fresh water wells. Wabi was saddened by the memory of the violence he had seen among the humans.

    The old man's hair was long and white. His body tall, thin, and agile. He was much happier in the presence of the animals that inhabited this world. He particularly enjoyed watching the wild horses, called Marsh Tackies, gamboling in the marsh grass. He even had a Tacky stallion he enjoyed riding. The horses thrived on the tender green grass of the marsh. Wabi communicated freely with them simply by calmly looking into their eyes. *Humans are so limited,* he thought, because they typically looked without seeing and heard without listening. The animals and one other main source of information kept the old man advised concerning human and other animal activity in the area. That other source of information came from plants. For example, he could lay his hands on the bark of a 300-year-old Live Oak and learn what it had experienced in all those years. It was beyond understanding how the animal and plant kingdoms had evolved to perfection and left mankind to deal with their violence and paranoia.

Wabi arrived in this place long ago from a universe outside the earth's space and time. It would be centuries before this species speculated that there was a probability that infinite universes existed.

A theory they would call "The String Theory" would predict infinite universes existed, therefore allowing for infinite possibilities. Instant travel through and between the universes could be triggered by a single concentrated thought which rendered the speed of light's 186,400 miles per second obsolete.

Intelligent life in all of these worlds was a rare phenomenon. The elders of Wabi's world predicted the possibility of another universe with intelligent life on a small planet circling a medium sized star in a spiral galaxy. So. as others before him had done, he arrived in a place that may one day produce advanced life. His sole mission was to nurture the evolution of that life.

The old man lived in a solid coquina block house. The stone was indigenous to the area, made of millions upon millions of tiny seashells and was not found elsewhere on the planet. It was a remarkable material, able to absorb cannon balls, was easy to be shaped with a saw, and was much lighter than granite or marble. It was also impregnable to the forces of the tropical cyclones, which usually arrived in early fall.

His furniture was all handmade from the red cedar, cypress, and Live Oak trees that thrived in the area. He was a master potter of considerable skill. Exquisite, handmade, carved clay vessels were scattered throughout the rooms. The house was in the center of a large Live Oak hammock, where Wabi walked daily.

Standing in the center of the hammock felt like being in a magnificent cathedral. Some of Wabi's food came from his small garden, supplemented by hickory nuts, acorns, and three varieties of grapes (muscadine, fox, and scuppernong). His wine was produced from the muscadine grapes and the tidal creeks teemed with fish, oysters, and clams. He was provided with plenty of fish in the warm summers by schools of porpoise who arrived in the creek outside his house. Their feeding frenzy forced scores of mullet up onto the bank.

Human intruders were not a problem because the hammock was invisible to all but a few, and those few were so rare he had only met a handful in all these years. Just as butterflies can see into the infrared spectrum—which is invisible to humans—so it was that the hammock was totally invisible to most humans. He called his home "The Hide."

The Hide

Young Samuel

Samuel Worley Faver

My father's name was Samuel Worley Faver and he was born in St. Augustine, Florida, on September 13, 1904. He sometimes said the bad luck he had experienced in his life was from being born on Friday the thirteenth.

He had four siblings: three brothers and one sister. His mother's name was Florida Ellen Dykes, and she died from tuberculosis at the age of thirty-four.

When my grandmother died, my grandfather was devastated by her death and never fully recovered. After this loss, the care and raising of the four youngest children fell to the oldest child, my Uncle Hiram Faver. When he was only nineteen years old, he had to raise and care for his brothers and a sister. Our family has always said that Uncle Hiram never married because he had already raised a family.

While Grandmother lived, she did an excellent job of caring for the entire family. Grandfather was a St. Johns County Commissioner and successful business man with a large shop on Riberia Street in St. Augustine where he cared for horses (before automobiles), and built carriages and wagons. It was a large operation and included blacksmith and farrier shops.

Grandfather's favorite friend and hunting companion was Dr. George Worley, one of the few doctors in St. Johns County. Dr. Worley and Grandfather would take an annual hunting trip south to Pellicer Creek, which is the southern boundary of the county. Grandfather loved riding his Marsh Tacky stallion on these trips. The Marsh Tackies were indigenous ponies that lived in the North Florida marshes. Sadly, our federal government in all its wisdom saw fit to kill all of the Tackies, because it was thought they spread ticks among the Florida cattle.

My father was named after Dr. Worley and the name has come down for over 100 years to me. Dr. Worley probably saved my father's life when he was severely injured in a wagon accident. His brother, Ray, was driving a horse and wagon too fast around a street corner and it overturned. Uncle Ray was thrown clear, but my father was thrown into a spinning wagon wheel, causing very serious head, back, and right wrist injuries. Dr. Worley took care of my father's wounds.

After Grandmother's death, Samuel moved to Jacksonville to work in his uncle's grocery store. Dad enrolled in Duval High School while he was working and completed the tenth grade. He then married my mother, Birdie DeGrove. He was a wonderful father to my sister Jackie, and me!

Travels

Thanks to my oldest son, Keith, and my working life, I have traveled this world. Following are four of my favorite places:

Stonehenge

In 1990 Dena and I flew to London to visit our dear Virginia friends Lee and Emily. Em was a government attorney handling legal matters for the U.S. government and the Scandinavian Airlines. Lee was a U.S. Navy commander directing aircraft in the Middle East during the "Desert Storm" operation.

One day we decided to travel to Stonehenge because all of us were interested in seeing the ancient stones. Dena and I had no idea what lay in store for us. We arrived at the Stonehenge site in the early afternoon and were very fortunate because we were virtually alone during our visit.

We walked across a lovely green pasture to get closer to the magnificent stones, which looked like the ruins of an ancient cathedral. Then we went over a little rise in the land and gazed down at the stones. I was immediately overcome with a deep feeling of sadness and tears began running down my cheeks. I turned and saw that Dena was also sobbing. Lee and Emily caught up with us and could not believe our spontaneous reactions.

We gained control and walked to the little Salisbury Cathedral on the site grounds. During the walk we were hit again with a synchronistic event. As I walked along, I glanced down and saw an unusual piece of stone at my feet. I immediately said aloud, "chert." Emily turned and asked, "What did you say?" I said, "This is a shard of chert." Em asked, "How do you know that?" I said, "I have never in my life seen stone like this, but when I held it in my hand, the word "chert" immediately came into my mind. Investigation later proved that the shard was indeed, chert. The piece now resides in a 1,200-year-old piece of pottery on the fireplace mantle in our Palm Valley cabin.

Shard of Chert

Machu Picchu

In 2017 my oldest son, Keith, and I flew to Lima, Peru, and caught another flight to Cusco, where we stayed for three days in the Monasterio Hotel. The hotel and grounds were formerly an ancient monastery. Much of the art and furnishings dated back many, many years. We spent our days walking the old steep streets of Cusco.

Machu Picchu

This was good conditioning for us because the elevation of Cusco is 11,000+ feet.

After three days, we were picked up in a trekking company van and transported to the beginning of our trail through the Andes. We walked fifty miles in six days across the Andes following ancient Inca mountain

trails reaching an elevation of 15,218 feet. We reached Agua Caliente on the sixth day of our trek. Next morning we were transported to Machu Piccu. The first look at the ancient city is almost overwhelming. We seemed to feel in our bones the sacredness of those old buildings. There were very

Center of Machu Picchu

few tourists around, so we truly enjoyed the experience.

My favorite building was called "The Temple of the Sun," which had a stone slab table in the middle of the room. The table was aligned so that the holy men could predict and track the solstices by the angle of the sunbeams coming through the window opening and striking the surface of the table. Later we were transported by train back to Cusco—a beautiful mountain train ride.

Keith and I still talk about those magical days!!

Antarctica

One morning in January 2020, Keith calls and says, "Dad, ya want to go down to Antarctica for a visit?" I said, "Sure, when are we leaving?" He replied, "I have us a flight booked next week."

So the following week Keith, his daughter, Chloe, Keith's business partner, Jim Gray, and I arrived in Buenos Aires, Argentina. After spending the night there, we were bussed to Ushuaia at the southernmost tip of South America. We boarded the National Geographic Expedition ship, "Orion," and departed.

We spent the first night crossing the infamous "Drake Passage." The waves must have been huge because the ship was moving up and down all night. The morning found us in the Weddell Sea and we saw our first iceberg. By the end of the day, we began to see many more, some as big as an office building.

There were huge glaciers on shore calving off bergs over 100 feet thick. The weather was beautiful as we acclimated to moving from winter to summer in one week. Each day's schedule was announced by the captain over the ship's speakers.

Snow Covered Mountains

Most days we went ashore to mingle with tremendous numbers of wildlife.

One of the locations was home to an estimated 1,000,000+ penguins. We saw leopard seals and had a close encounter with a humpback whale who, when seeing us, sounded within twenty yards of our Zodiac. I was very happy keeping up with everyone from the rocky beaches because my total right knee replacement was only a little over a year old.

Of course, my personal favorite place on the ship was the lounge. I always woke up ahead of our group, so I would go directly to the lounge for coffee. As I was the oldest passenger, the wonderful folks in the lounge quickly began addressing me as "Pops." When I walked in my friends would say, "Good Morning, Pops. Do ya want cappuccino or a latte this morning?" Of course, in the afternoon when I walked in they would say, "Hey Pops, here's your Bulleit Old Fashioned."

One morning our *Norwegian Lady* Captain announced, "Today we will make available a Polar Plunge for anyone who is interested." Of course, our whole group signed up right away, but we noticed there were very few other signees on the list.

Keith, Chloe, Jim, and I showed up on the ship's stern in the early afternoon. There was a light snow falling, huge ice bergs were floating nearby and the water was 30°F. The national geographic crew was wearing their heavy cold weather gear.

Keith, Chloe, and Worley

So three generations of the Faver family lined up holding hands. Keith gave Chloe and me a quick kiss and we dove off the stern. Chloe was very quick to get out of the water and the crew members wrapped her in a warm towel as she came up the ladder. Keith and I enjoyed a leisurely swim before we came out. What a great day!

We spent a week cruising the Weddell Sea, enjoying the icebergs and animals. The weather was pristine. Of course, we all read *Endurance, Shackleton's Incredible Voyage* by Alfred Lansing before we left home. It was fascinating to personally see some of the sites he stayed at during the historic saving of his crew after their ship was crushed by the sea ice

Then it was back north across the Drake and to Ushuaia, then a long flight home through Santiago,

Chile. I don't believe I will ever surpass the joy of this journey with my children!

Israel

In 1998 I traveled to Israel to inspect body armor that my employer was manufacturing with our Israeli friends. At that time, I was the Director of Quality Assurance for a large international manufacturing company specializing in body armor. Upon completion, the 5,000 armored vests would be sold to the Turkish police. Earlier I had made two inspection trips to Bucharest, Romania, to inspect the vests which would hold the ballistic panels.

I flew from Jacksonville to Newark and then to Frankfurt to catch an El Al flight to Tel Aviv. During this flight and the days in Israel I was amazed at the efficiency of Israel's security personnel. When I boarded the plane in Munich, there was a young man in a very nice gray suit and tie making eye contact with every passenger as we boarded the plane. I am sure that no terrorist with harmful intentions would get by this young man.

When we landed in Tel Aviv, I was walking through the terminal to claim my baggage when an alarm went off. Within a few seconds the entire terminal was empty except for me. I stayed because I wanted to personally see what happened next. I could see a light flashing atop one of the baggage scanners and I stepped behind a concrete column for protection. Then six young men in suits and ties ran by me toward the scanner. As they ran, they were pulling Uzi's from under their coats. Thank God it was a false alarm and none of these brave young men were injured.

I gathered my bags and walked out of the terminal where a driver was waiting for me. We drove north to my hotel on the Sea of Galilee. As soon as I checked in, I walked down to the water's edge of the sea. I stared out across the lake and far away on the other shore I could see the Golan Heights in Syria. As I stared at the water, my mind went back to the time Jesus walked on this water and saved Peter from drowning. I cupped some of that precious water in my hands and sent up a thank you prayer.

The next morning I reported to the manufacturing plant which was not far across the desert. I spent an unforgettable week with the team producing the vests. Their testing facility was underground and state of the art. The test panels stopped the bullets exactly as they were designed. The Quality Assurance Manager opened his safe and let me inspect the weapons he had used in the last war. I especially liked his side arm, which was a .44 magnum Desert Eagle. Of course, every person in Israel is connected to the military.

One day the plant manager said, "Worley, take the afternoon off. There's a site in the desert we want you to visit."

My driver was a young lady from Fort Lauderdale. She was eighteen years old and was in the Army Reserve. One day she told her parents, "I need to go home to Israel." She went to the plant store and bought me a hat, because she said I could not go into the desert bareheaded. I still have that hat.

We drove into the desert where the temperature that day was 114°F. We arrived at an ancient Roman stadium, which looked like a miniature coliseum. I sat in the old stone seat and wondered what went on in that arena all those years ago.

On Saturday the plant manager said, "You cannot come to Israel without seeing Jerusalem!" Very soon my driver and I were driving down the Jordanian border toward the holy city. All along the border was a mine field and Israeli soldiers driving open jeeps with mounted .50 caliber machine guns.

I had forgotten how old Jerusalem really is with its stone walls, David's Tomb, and a remnant of the foundation from Solomon's Temple. I could only stay in the Holocaust Museum for a few moments because I was overcome with sadness as I walked in the entrance.

The Wailing Wall was my favorite site. The wall is ancient and huge and there were many people praying at the wall and placing little slips of paper containing printed messages to God in the cracks of the wall. I went to the wall to kneel and pray but not before someone gave me a Yakima to cover my head. What a wonderful, spiritual day I will never forget.

After a week with these very special people in this historical place, I returned to America and my family, feeling very blessed for the experiences of my trip. I learned a week later that a bomb exploded very near my hotel in Galilee.

The Guana

The Guana

I have shared stories of the Guana in another book, but much of my youth in the late 1940's and early 1950's was spent hunting, trapping wild hogs, and taking long horseback rides in this beautiful landscape. Formerly, the eastern side of the Guana was like a meadow with the headwaters of the Guana River flowing through Ponte Vedra from the St. Johns County line to join the Matanzas River. Many years ago there was a connection with the ocean at the county line. This narrow cut into the ocean was called Carter's Run. When my Grandpa Willie would drive his Model T pickup to Pablo (now Jacksonville Beach) from Palm Valley, he would have to drive through a little salt water at Carter's Run during high tide.

On the eastern side of the Guana, we would shoot Green Winged Teal, wild hogs, and usually a few large moccasins and rattlesnakes.

A dam was built across the Guana Creek and joined the east and west shores in 1957. The eastern side joined the shore near what was still called the old Coast Guard Station. This facility housed barracks for the Coast Guard unit patrolling and protecting the ocean front during WWII.

I remember the Coast Guard lookout towers at intervals along the beach from St. Augustine north to the St. Johns County line. We would see the armed men patrolling the shoreline with German Shepard dogs. Even so, a German U-boat was successful in unloading several spies one night. In a few days, they were apprehended and relieved of their explosives. Then they were all hanged.

I will stop here with the old war stories, but there are other incidents that I can recall.

After Mr. Stockton completed the dam, the meadow was covered and a lake was created. My friend, Flavian, and I used to hunt just west of the dam in what was called

Booth's Hammock at that time. There was a large open, grassy, mostly dry, lake area north of Shell Bluff, which was called The Big Savanna. We brought the dogs and chased the largest wild boar we ever saw into the Savanna one day, but the dogs lost his scent when he entered the shallow water.

We stopped and ate our lunch of Vienna sausage, saltines, and water. As we ate, we looked to the east side of the lake and the monster boar came out of the woods and stretched out in the cool water. His tusks were so long they curved up almost into his eyes. He had already cut one of the dogs badly, so we just called it a day. When we got home, Merlin sewed up the wounded dog with needle and thread and within a week he was healing fast.

Flavian showed me something very interesting one day. Just east of the Savanna, in a fairly clear area among the little scrub oaks he pointed out some large conch shells that had been arranged in an orderly manner. He said, "William, there's a grave under each one of these shells. This is the old Booth Family Graveyard." Sadly, my mentor and best friend, Flavian, is gone to the other side now.

There was one other interesting place in the Guana, north of the dam, and was always referred to as "Where Arthur hung the Hawk." I never knew until over sixty years later in a conversation with my old friend, Raymond Mickler, the true story of this place. I always thought that someone had killed a hawk in this place and hung it in a tree, but it was much more significant than that. It seems there was an outlaw long ago called "The Hawk." Apparently, Arthur and his neighbors caught and hanged him one day. So this place forevermore became known as, "Where Arthur hung The Hawk!"

I recall one day when the usual Palm Valley crew parked on the dam and we turned the dogs loose to stir up some wild hogs. It was a beautiful clear and cool fall day. I was riding Flavian's horse, King, who was a big, strong, white gelding. King and I hunted north along the Guana shore and lost track of time. Before I knew it, the sun was setting and we were many miles north of the dam. The trail back south was very dim in the moonlight, so I decided to just trust King and give him his head. I leaned forward on his mane to avoid low hanging branches. King was very fast for his size, and we were soon headed south at a gallop with tree limbs sometimes brushing my back.

When King and I arrived at the dam, there was Flavian and the boys worrying and waiting for me. Flavian said, "I was worried about ya, William, until way north I could barely hear King galloping back to us. That sure was a welcome sound, and then I could see that white horse flashing down the shore in the moonlight." I will never forget the boys lined up on the dam waiting for me and King and the smile on Flavian's face.

The Legend of Connie

(The following story may not be enjoyed by everyone. You must bear in mind that this true story goes back to a different time—sixty-two years ago.)

In 1960, I went into business with Dena's father and brother. We named our partnership "Duval Farms." It was situated on Papa's 250 acres in West Jacksonville on Collins Road. In fact, Collins in that day was dirt as it entered Papa's property and reached a dead end at our hog pens.

This part of Jacksonville was very rural then. The piece of property had beautiful old oaks and a creek that ran thru the swamp.

We were the second largest hog farm in Florida with 3,000+ head of hogs. The Davis family in Dade County was the largest at that time. We also had a few horses and a small herd of Black Angus cattle, around 300 head.

In the next ten years, Papa Grover became one of the best friends I have ever known. He completely restored the house Dena was raised in and we lived there from 1960 to 1969. It was situated on the eastern boundary of the family property.

Sometimes late at night, we would hear a shotgun go off over toward the swamp, where some old abandoned houses sat rotting.

I asked Dena's brother, Clifford, if he was shooting coons at night. He replied, "The shots come from Connie's house. I learned that Connie's house was the old, deserted house down near the creek in the swamp that ran through the farm.

Apparently, everyone nearby knew about Connie. Clifford shared her tale with me. You have to understand this was long ago and country boys with fast cars usually got together on Saturday night to have a drink or three and discuss beautiful southern girls.

Clifford and his friends would see an unsuspecting city boy come into the bar and one of the friends would go over and engage the fellow in conversation. This would usually lead to a discussion about pretty girls. The conversation would eventually lead to beautiful, available girls and Connie would be mentioned. She was presented as a lonesome, beautiful girl out in the country and she may be available if properly approached.

So, the boys arrive out at the farm to a dark house in the swamp with the latest Connie candidate. Clifford would usually lead the young man up the path to the front porch. As he goes up the steps, a man with a shotgun rushes out of the front door. He screams, "You will never have my daughter again!" Then he fires the 12-gauge shotgun. Clifford grabs his chest and falls back into the front yard.

The young man thinks Clifford is dead and runs for his life. He runs out of the woods and finds a dirt road to escape. He sees a light from a house under oak trees near our farm. He runs through the yard and makes it to the backdoor and goes straight into the house without knocking.

Dena's mother, Granny Punk, was up early and in the kitchen preparing food for our Sunday family lunch the next day. The poor city boy fell down on her kitchen floor and said, 'They have killed Clifford at the old house in the swamp!"

The young man was horrified to see my dear mother-in-law start laughing. She said, "You must have met Miss Connie."

Every few weeks, we would hear the shot and feel sorry for another young man.

Imagination

Leonardo da Vinci, Carl Jung, Albert Einstein, and Stephen Hawking—all great minds with wondrous imaginations and intellect have always fascinated me. I have encouraged my grandchildren to probe their imagination and find the treasures that reside there.

I remember traveling down US-1 south of St. Augustine years ago with my grandchildren pointing out the David Johnson fast food restaurant, which almost never had a car in the parking lot. I told them that actually it was the entrance to a Wormhole, where people were able to travel instantly to other universes. Then one day the old restaurant was gone.

One day I was taking my usual weekly five-mile walk south of the Palm Valley bridge when I noticed an abandoned house back in the woods and immediately recognized it as the next Wormhole, even imagining a being standing at the missing front door and staring out at this world. The old house is a perfect Wormhole entrance almost obscured from human sight in its vines and overhanging tree branches. Each summer it almost disappears in its camouflage of vines and bushes.

This is the sort of free imaginative thinking I have encouraged in my grandchildren. One only has to study the lives of the geniuses mentioned in the first paragraph to see that this fable is not so farfetched.

Palm Valley Wormhole

Leonardo's imaginative thinking was unprecedented during his time, resulting in amazing works of art. Sigmund Freud separated from his adopted son, Carl Jung, because of Carl's study and belief in supernatural occurrences.

Einstein's theories concerning the nature of light and relativity were at first unacceptable during his time, and Hawking's theories concerning "infinite universes" are still not accepted in some quarters. All of these great thinkers had one thing in common. They had absolutely free imaginations.

If during this long life of mine I am able to help my grandchildren approach this wondrous reality with open minds and active imaginations, I will leave this beautiful world perfectly happy!

Milton

Milton Faver

Milton Faver's life in America began like my branch of the Faver family who immigrated to Greenville, Georgia before the American Revolution, but he went west to St. Louis, Missouri instead. He fought a duel in a street of St. Louis, and when he saw the man fall to the ground he knew he must leave town and go far away as quickly as possible.

He did not stop riding until he found himself across the border in Monterrey, Mexico. After some time he moved back into America with his Mexican wife and settled near Cibola, Texas, which is near the present Big Bend National Park.

Apparently, the Missouri Posse had long since given up on finding him, so he settled on the land and began to build his ranch. The first years were enjoyable as he worked his cattle and raised his children.

Fort Davis was located nearby, manned by the U.S. Army, so Milton and his family had protection from the savage Apaches in that region. But then in 1862, the fort was abandoned by the Army as they went to fight the Southern Rebels.

Milton built his own adobe fort to protect his family and ranch hands. During these difficult years he was wounded twice by the hostiles. The fort that he built saved everyone from massacre by the Apaches.

After the Civil War ended, Fort Davis was reactivated and Milton began to build a thriving cattle operation. These were good years for all his growing family and ranch hands. In a few years his cattle herd was healthy and growing and he was able to begin selling feeder calves. It is said that during his calf sales he would stand at the gate as the animals went to their new owners. Milton would collect the payment in gold coins and drop them into a leather pouch held in his hand. He would also drive his finished steers to the Kansas City cattle processing plant to sell.

Milton was recognized as the first true cattle baron in Texas history, and when he passed away his herd exceeded 10,000 head.

Note: Much of this story can be verified. The University of Texas has published the story of Milton Faver on line. The only missing link in their story was they could not confirm where Milton came from before the duel in St. Louis. After they see this story, they will learn that his family landed in Virginia in 1634, and settled in Culpepper County.

The location of Milton's 30,000-acre ranch has become a historic site. His fort still stands in Texas and has many visitors every year. It is on this old man's bucket list to visit this place before he closes his eyes for good.

Trailer Trash

My son, Keith, and his son, Kasey, flew to New Orleans with a few friends to attend an SEC football game between the LSU Tigers and the Florida Gators. Keith rented a long black limousine for the day and they headed north up the Mississippi to Baton Rouge. Kasey and his friends were all dressed in coveralls and no shirts, wearing "Gator" orange and blue caps. The Gators were on top of their game that day and soundly thrashed the Tigers.

Casey and friend at the game

After the game they are outside the stadium walking to the car when Kasey feels something strike his lower leg.

He turned and was astonished to see an elderly lady in a motorized wheel chair that had intentionally rammed his leg. The man walking behind her was probably her son and he said, "Don't pay no attention to them Granny, they're just trailer trash." So, the boys got into their limo as their chauffeur held the door.

God Bless Our Police Officers

Our family has been so blessed in our contacts with police officers over the years. The following are a few of these encounters:

My youngest son, Kevin, has always loved fishing. In his early teens I introduced him to two of my oldest friends, Captain Wimpy Sutton and Captain Mike Scanlan, two of the most famous offshore/inshore fishing charter captains working out of Mayport.

When he was fifteen years old, I bought him a 17-foot jon boat and trailer and an old Ford pickup. So, early one morning he was headed to Mayport for a day of fishing. Unfortunately, he had forgotten to hook up the safety chain between the trailer and truck. Bad mistake!

He was driving in south Jacksonville Beach on Third Street, when he hit a little bump in the road and the trailer jumped off the truck hitch and went in its own direction. The boat and trailer passed the truck and crossed the intersection at 16th Avenue South into the southbound lane. The trailer came to a halt directly in front of a Jacksonville Beach police cruiser. The policemen walked over to Kevin and says, "Morning, son. Where ya headed?" Kevin says, "Morning, sir. I'm headed to Mayport for a day of fishing." So, the officer says, "Let's get this trailer back on the hitch!"

So they walk the boat and trailer back to the truck and put it back on the hitch and FASTENED the safety chain. The officer said, "Have a good day, buddy. Hope ya catch some fish," and drove away! All this before Kevin was old enough for a driver's license.

~~

One day while we were living in west Jacksonville in the 1960's, Dena was twenty-five and our daughter, Cindy, was four years old. They were headed north on Ricker Road to Lake Shore and Dena was driving too fast. They were pulled over by a Duval County police officer. The officer walked up to the car window and pulled out his ticket book with pen in hand and started to write; he had not noticed Cindy taking a nap in the back seat.

Cindy woke up, sees the officer writing and immediately starts loudly crying and screams, "Oh no! Please don't take my mommy to jail!" The officer tore up the ticket and drove away.

~~

We went to the Florida Theatre in downtown Jacksonville for a nice evening listening to Willie Nelson. We were standing in the ticket line, but somehow I became separated from Keith and Dena with about five people between us.

Keith called over a Jacksonville Policeman and says, "Officer, see that old man up there in line? He's my father and I 'll bet he has his pocket knife. And he may not get it back if security takes it. If you can get it from him, I'll walk it back to the car."

So I was minding my own business and got a tap on my shoulder. There stands a sharp looking police officer. He says, "Mr. Faver, are you carrying your knife tonight?" I reached in my pocket and said, "Doggone it, I forgot it tonight." The young officer says, "Good," and walked away!

~~

One morning I was driving north on 9th Street in Jacksonville Beach in my 4X4 Ford truck, when I saw blue lights in the mirror. I pulled over and a young Jacksonville Beach policeman walked up to my window with his ticket book in hand. He looked at my license and said, "Mr. Faver, do you know how fast you were driving?" I said "No sir, I guess I don't even know the speed limit on 9th Street." He said, "I'm not even going to write your speed on this ticket." I said, "Thank you sir. I was born here in 1937 and have been driving this street all these years and have never known the speed limit."

I could tell the young officer was calculating how old I was and thinking, "*Man, this old boy is really older than dirt.*" He handed me a warning citation and said, "You don't need to do anything with this ticket. You can tear it up if you want to." I wished that young man a nice day and he drove away!

Thank God for all our police officers!

Bragging Rights

I suppose all of us like to brag on ourselves now and then. An old man once said, "Son, ya might as well brag on yourself, cause no one else will." There was a day during my working life of 48 years that I am most proud of and here is the story:

In 1984 I was the sub-sea engineer/technician on a floating oil drilling rig, the Aleutian Key. She was a deep-water offshore drilling rig, 200´ wide by 250´ long. We were drilling about 300 miles southeast of Rio de Janeiro, Brasil, in the Atlantic Ocean. The previous month we had begun drilling and things were moving along well with the operation, so I came home to Florida for a month's rest. There is only one sub-sea hand on the rig at a time, so some of the work days could be forty hours long. Thank God for our Cajun cooks on board, because they would bring my meals out to me when I could not leave the drilling operation.

After a great month at home, I flew to Miami and caught a flight to Rio and then went by helicopter offshore to the rig. I did not know it yet, but I was in for a sad surprise after we landed on the rig. The sub-sea engineer I was replacing met us as we landed on the rig and quickly gave me the bad news. The rig had been out of operation for a week, and he had not been able to identify the problem. Petrobras, the multinational petroleum corporation that owns the well, had suspended their daily payment of $90,000

Aleutian Key

until we could regain the drilling operation. The bosses were not happy and the drilling superintendent was on his way from Houston headquarters. So I went right to work to try to find the problem. The superintendent landed the next morning and I had already been working 24 hours. By the time the boss arrived, I had found the problem and the rig was drilling. I will never forget what he said before he flew back to Houston. "Son, I have been in the oil business a long time and you are the best I have ever seen!" Mr. Johnny Farley, you will probably never see a copy of this little book, but thanks again for your kind words.

Note: We were so fortunate that this well turned out to be extremely successful and I believe truly helped my friends in Brasil.

The Farm Doctor

Papa Grover invited me to be his partner in the family hog/cattle farm in 1960. Of course, being an old Palm Valley country boy, I loved the offer and quit my job working in the Southern Bell Central Office in Jacksonville Beach. I was no stranger to hogs, but the ones I was used to were wild and wooly! We would catch them with our hog dogs and if they were females, we turned them loose. If they were boars, we would castrate them and turn them loose for next year's barbecue. If the dogs chased a barrow (castrated male from the prior year), we caught them and fed them corn for a while and then had a family and friends barbecue.

Papa's family farm hog population was always a little over 3,000 head. We would buy about 80-100 head of feeder pigs every week at livestock auction sales in Lake City, Madison, Gainesville, and Jacksonville. At our farm every week, semi-truck/trailers would pick up finished #1 (240+ pounds) hogs for processing at the old Jones-Chambliss plant in Jacksonville.

The farm animals' health was my responsibility as Papa believed we would never have to call a veterinarian, because, "Son can take care of the animals."

There used to be a business in Jacksonville named Poultry Health Service, so that is where I purchased all of our medical supplies, i.e., antibiotics (both injectable and water soluble for the animals' drinking water).

I was also responsible for medicating the farm dogs, including giving annual rabies inoculations. If we had a mama cow lying down in the pasture with a calf that would not be born, I would go up inside her with my bare hand and arm, find those two little back legs and slowly pull that little one into his or her new world. Why I wasn't exposed to brucellosis or some other problem, the Lord only knows!

If a horse had a fistulous withers infection, I would give it penicillin injections. Castration of boars and bulls was carried out with a very sharp knife. Now that I look back, I can remember the castration blade on my Case XX knife blade was inscribed, "For Flesh Only!"

I realize during our present times these activities sound barbaric, but we did what was necessary back then with what we had to work with. The time was sixty plus years ago.

The Mountain Sorcerer

My oldest son, Keith, calls one day and says, "Pops let's go to Peru and walk from Cuzco to Manchu Piccu." I said "When do we leave?" and he said, "Next week we'll fly to Lima and then to Cuzco." So, we had one of the most special times of my life!

We made it to that ancient mountain city 11,000+ feet above sea level and stayed in an old-old hotel, the Monesterio. One morning our van arrived and took us to the beginning of our fifty mile walk over the Andes.

After three days of trekking, we arrived at a glacier lake. A few hours prior to our arrival at the lake, this old man was behind the others and a little tired. As I walked up that old Inca rocky path, I heard beautiful flute music behind me. I turned and saw two interesting looking people walking behind me. Their music seemed to invigorate me and I was climbing with renewed energy. They followed me to the Lake, where I learned these folks were a sorcerer and his apprentice. We joined my group and sat down on the shore of a beautiful Alpine lake with a glacier emptying into the water from the snow covered peak above. Keith asked our guide what the temperature of the lake was and if anyone had ever taken a swim. The guide said the water temperature was about 35°F and several people had tried to take a swim, with the record for staying in that frigid water being seven minutes.

So Keith strips down and walks out into the water and stays for 20 minutes. The amazing thing is that toward the end of his dip we heard a noise from the mountain that sounded like thunder, but it turned out to be an avalanche far up the mountain. So Keith came ashore pretty chilly and dressed.

The sorcerer said he would like to perform a ceremony in honor of the mountain allowing our presence. At his direction we gathered in a circle and he spread a lovely small blanket with us sitting around. He produced a little bag and started spreading small colorful pebbles in the middle of the blanket. Using the Inca tongue, he gave a short dedication to the mountain. We asked him what the little colored pebbles were and he said, "They are sugar pebbles, because the mountain gods love sugar." He then folded the blanket around the sugar pebbles and said he had a special place to bury them on the mountain.

I will never forget that day and the kindness of the mountain sorcerer.

Palm Valley Winter School Days

Back during the old days in Palm Valley (1940's), we had really cold winters. The school bus picked us up at the old school house in front of Palm Valley Baptist Church, which took us north to Jacksonville Beach Elementary. On those cold mornings I always did something that would be unheard of today! I would bring a few pieces of split oak wood and a little handful of fat wood and have a little fire going before my few schoolmates arrived. They could now warm themselves.

My father and I would go into the woods every Saturday during the winter and gather firewood for the two large fireplaces in The Big House. It was my job, when I got off the school bus in the afternoons, to split lighter knots of fat pine and carry oak back logs and stack them on the front porch for fires the next cold morning.

Dad and I would cut the oak logs with a two-man cross cut saw every Saturday. Looking back, I cannot imagine a better life than the one I had growing up! I guess that's why I love using the two fire places in our Palm Valley bungalow in the woods, and I can still swing an axe at eighty-five years old.

Birdie

My mother was truly a remarkable woman! I suppose it was in her genes to help other people and love our America. Her name was Mary Birdie DeGrove and her father called her his little "May Bird" as she was born May 9th, 1910.

Her father, William Morton DeGrove, was a St. Johns County commissioner and served two terms in the Florida Legislature. During his political career he championed women's rights and tried unsuccessfully to pass bills for women's rights during his two legislative terms. Thankfully the women's rights bill was passed after Grandpa left the Legislature.

I remember Mama giving child care classes for young pregnant women. The classes were held in the little red school house across the road from the Palm Valley Baptist Church. I was a little blue eyed, blonde boy at that time and I went to class with her every day. She used my little skinny body to demonstrate the proper way to fit a diaper.

When World War II was upon us and we had lots of German U-Boat activity off our coast in north Florida, there was concern in our government that the Germans may send airplanes to bomb one of the several military bases located in our area.

This was prior to the wide use of radar, so the government asked for volunteers living near the coast to act as airplane spotters and identify aircraft coming across the coast. Of course, my mother was one of the first volunteers. Each morning she would drive south to the Palm Valley bridge across the Intracoastal Waterway, which was operated by the United States Corps of Engineers. A class was conducted by the government to educate the volunteers in identifying aircraft, specifically planes of the Luftwaffe. When Mama would arrive every morning at the bridge, there were binoculars and a radio/telephone available for her use. Thank God, she never identified a hostile aircraft.

I still have Mama's old government issued arm band from those days.

Mary Birdie DeGrove Faver's Observer Arm Band

I will never forget Mama standing in the kitchen crying when she heard on our little battery-operated radio that President Franklin Delano Roosevelt had died.

Dreams

Carl Jung, the world-famous psychiatrist who made amazing discoveries regarding our dream world, would surely not be surprised by this story!

I have been a dreamer my entire life. The first dream work I did happened when I was very young. I grew up in the stone and cypress house that my grandfather built in the latter part of the 1890's. It is called "The Big House" in our family and still stands. Located in the midst of huge Live Oaks draped with long strands of Spanish moss, it surely is a magical, dreamy place.

I vividly remember those years when I was about six years old. It was about that time when I seemed to wake up to the world around me. I remember wanting to write a novel concerning the war that our nation was fighting in 1943. The first sentence was as far as I got – "The Bombs were bursting on the battlefield that night." Next,

I was building model airplanes and ships out of wood and paper.

Also around this time is when my lifelong dream work started. I was troubled by a recurring dream that involved being chased by a hideous monster; thank goodness I woke up before I was caught. One night the monster was chasing me to the edge of a cliff that fell away for about 1,000 feet. When I reached the edge, instead of waking up I dove off the cliff, spread my arms and FLEW, leaving the monster behind. I have been able to fly in my dreams now for almost eighty years.

The most interesting flight made in my dream work was a result of reading all of the Carlos Castaneda novels concerning the sorcerer, Don Juan, who routinely taught his apprentices to fly on demand in their dreams.

The old myth concerning sorcerer dream flights is that they were able to travel in their dreams and inflict actual physical harm to their enemies. I was in my mid-thirties when I read Castaneda's work. I was fascinated by this concept and set out to master dream travel.

Don Juan's first step in learning dream travel was to be able to look at your hands at will in your dreams. For about six months I went to sleep reminding myself that I needed of see my hands in my dream that night. And then one night it happened. I simply said "I need to look at my hands," and looked down and there they were! I felt like a new door had opened to my sub-conscience. So, always pushing the envelope, I decided to take this new practice to another level. I thought, *"If I can successfully see my hands, why can't I take control of my dreams and fly through the sky at night?"* God help me, it worked! So several times a week, I flew in my dreams on demand around our neighborhood and even out over the ocean. Then I decided to give this new activity the ultimate Don Juan Test!

At this time we were still in the cattle business with a herd of woods cattle and our horses in what is now the Guana Preserve. My plan was to dream travel to my favorite place in these 1,000's of acres. The place was called Bobcat Point and lies at the headwaters of Jones Creek. I would ride my quarter horse, Fancy, to Bobcat Point, arrange some oyster shells into a specific pattern, and that night return in my dream and rearrange the pattern. The next day I would ride back and see if I was successful in changing the pattern in my dream.

So Fancy and I rode to Bobcat Point and arranged about fifteen oyster shells in a circle on the creek bank. That night I went to sleep and had no trouble with my dream travel. I was flying along looking at the dark trees of Palm Valley in the moonlight when I had a very disturbing thought, *"What if I ride Fancy to Bobcat Point tomorrow in the daylight and see that the oyster shells have been rearranged, as I intended, from a circle to a cross?"*

I wondered as I flew, what my mental reaction would be if this experiment was successful. I decided therein that I would not be able to handle this new-found power if I proved that this old myth was indeed the truth! So, I turned around in mid-air, flew back home and returned to my bed with my beautiful wife.

It is really interesting that I have never considered trying this experiment in my dreams again since that night, nor have I visited Bobcat Point!!

Angels

I have always said the greatest gift I ever received in this long life was my wife, Dena. In just a few days we will celebrate our sixty-fifth wedding anniversary!

Her days revolve around me, three children, eight grandchildren and six great grandchildren. She remembers every birthday, knows everyone's needs and helps them in every way she can.

She has put up with this old man for sixty-five years and continues to be my inspiration and main reason for living. When I think of angels on this earth, it is she and all the women like her, who continually nurtures mankind.

Da Vinci and many of the greatest male artists continually painted the human female form because there is no doubt that form is the greatest art of all. Joan of Arc, Mother Teresa, and their counterparts throughout history make our male heroes dim by comparison.

I had the most vivid and inspiring dream not long ago, when I was visited by an angelic vision. Her beautiful face slowly materialized before me as she looked in my face with the kindest eyes I have ever seen. I cannot possibly describe the peaceful feeling her steady gaze filled me with. My dear mother would say, "If the Lord made anything better than a good woman, he kept it to himself."

My Therapy

Driving to Publix this morning to buy eggs and bacon for breakfast—and wine for later in the day—my heart is very, very, heavy due to the news we received last week. The all-time love of my life for over sixty-five years has a very serious illness. Mayo Clinic is on top of it, but the outcome may be unbelievably sad.

As I was driving to the store, I passed the old cow pen area in the Guana Preserve where fifty years ago we would have our fall roundup to inspect our woods cattle herd and administer any medical treatment the herd might need. Always, when I ride by the cow pens, I holler out loud to all those Palm Valley cowboys who have passed on to greener pastures, especially my best friend and partner, Flavian Mickler.

But this morning was very different because of my poor old suffering heart. I began to think of those wonderful days on horseback in those thousands of acres. My little quarter horse mare, Fancy, could always cheer me up, no matter how low I was. God help me I remember those rides with lunch in the saddle bag and my old dog, Buck, running beside me. No matter how troubled my mind was on those rides, I came home a new and better man. Rest in peace my dear friends, Fancy and Buck.

I got back home after this excellent mental therapy and fixed breakfast for my angel. We never know what the future holds. May God give us strength.

The End

If you would like to learn more about early 20th century life in Palm Valley, check out my other books in the Palm Valley series available in paperback and digital format at Amazon.com.

https://amazon.com/dp/1943369054

https://amazon.com/dp/1943369186

Made in the USA
Columbia, SC
25 October 2022

70015867R00050